# Rocket Fuel for Dreamers

Poems by Jordan Chaney

Edited by Joslyn Hamilton

**ROCKET FUEL FOR DREAMERS**

Poems by Jordan Chaney

 Published in the United States by Etcetera Press, Richland, WA. 

ISBN: 9781936824175
LCCN: 2012954915

For more information
or to contact Jordan Chaney:
jordanchaneypoet@gmail.com
www.billowingwords.com

*To my son David,*

*this is me, fighting the bears...*

# CONTENTS

Dedication .......... v
Acknowledgements .......... viii
Foreword by Patricia Briggs .......... ix

For Hard Times By Orian Baker .......... 1
Note to the Dreamer .......... 2
Time Machine .......... 3
Love Poem .......... 4
Rocket Fuel for Dreamers .......... 9
Fourth Dimension .......... 10
A Childlike Wonder .......... 11
Epitome of Impossible .......... 17
The Ninja Turtle Poem .......... 21
Conflict .......... 26
Conflicto .......... 31
Flowers for Monks .......... 36
Haiku for Mom .......... 41
Engines or Bodies or Wings .......... 42
The Drunken Sufi .......... 43
Letter to Liam .......... 47
I Cried .......... 52
Traffic Lights .......... 57
Light .......... 58
Immortal .......... 63
Forever Waiting .......... 64
A New Wine .......... 68

Apocalypse Haiku .......... 72
Ode to Grape .......... 73
Beyond the Crush .......... 77
Moonshine .......... 81
Goddess .......... 82
Warrior .......... 83
She's Fly .......... 86
Workin' My Way Up .......... 90
Pistol-Whipped .......... 94
Fortune .......... 95
TXT MSG for Her Insomnia .......... 99
Fly .......... 100
Another Gigantic Dream .......... 101
The Icarus Ode .......... 102
Yarn Haiku .......... 109
Notes on a Train to Big Sur .......... 110
Glossary .......... 118
Book Jordan Chaney .......... 142

## ACKNOWLEDGEMENTS

This book is possible because I have been fortunate in crossing paths with the following souls...

My mom, my son and Paris, Ernie Chapin, Patricia Briggs, Tommy Martin, TJ Martin, Andy Perdue, Ellen Tomaszewski, Thomas Braaten, Maisha Christian, Felicia Darwen, Diane Shepherd, Sergio Casteneda, Kim Dejong, Kristine Bono, Wendi Warner, Sarah Watkins, Orion Baker, Champagne Lewis, Mal Stewman, Lisa Jones, Sy Safransky, Ryan Jander, Matt & Michelle Price, Eric J. Johnson Ph.D., Joslyn Hamilton, Vanessa Fiola, Brian Seitz, Andra Day, David Garibaldi, Brett McKay

If I am forgetting anyone at all I promise to add your name to future reprints of this book!

## SPECIAL THANKS

Cover Art by Chase Dooley
Photography by Jenny Sanchez
Edited by Joslyn Hamilton
Translation by Kyle Black

## FOREWORD BY PATRICIA BRIGGS

For any writer, poetry is the most frightening of all the arts. To do it right requires bravery and a willingness to run naked in public. Polite poetry, clothed in acceptable thoughts and must-not-offend words, can sometimes be beautiful, whimsical or funny but is seldom worth a second read or more than a moment's consideration. Good poetry is scalding and wild and exposes the soul of the poet so it can better speak to our own.

A few years ago, when the master of ceremonies at our local writer's conference introduced Jordan Chaney and told us that he would read some of his poetry, I have to confess I wasn't expecting much. I may not be able to write it, but I love poetry traditional and modern–-and I know good stuff when I hear it. I also know how rare it is.

That day I glanced at the clock, settled in, and prepared to clap when it was over. But even in my pessimistic funk, I noticed something, some energy in the air. Many of the others in the crowd were hunched in their seats with carefully polite expressions. But there were a few people who shifted forward, their faces bright with anticipation. Maybe they were friends, I remember thinking, but the eagerness was too honest for obligation.

So I had a little warning when the poet began to speak.

Poetry is meant to be read aloud. Only when voiced does it reveal the full experience of rhythm and word. I felt like someone who had sat down to watch first graders tap-dance and Mikhail Baryshnikov [1] had taken the stage instead.

Jordan Chaney knows how to use words, how to play deftly with meanings, sounds and rhythm. But his poetry, like powerful art everywhere, surpasses mere skill: it is raw, huge, hopeful and naked.

Enjoy,

Patricia Briggs

---

[1] Mikhail Baryshnikov "Misha" is a Russian American dancer, choreographer and actor. He is known as one of the greatest ballet dancers in history.

## FOR HARD TIMES

the woman
who is missing an arm

and has a fly on her breast
that her daughter

who is missing a lip
is nursing from . . .

is
laughing

-Orion Baker, March/2006

*This poem is a snapshot of a moment my good friend Orion encountered while visiting a village near the Sobat River in Upper Nile State, Southern Sudan.

## NOTE TO THE DREAMER

at first
you kinda sorta gotta lie A LOT
you know, make it up
you kinda sorta gotta REALLY
disagree with the way
everything is now

get fed up

you really gotta let go and be free…
because somewhere
at some point
for some reason
you might've gave up and gave in

and we're here to fix that
we're here to fix that and each other

– Jordan

## TIME MACHINE

Cause I can see it now...
Way out in the far reaches of my finite
life; sixty or so years from today.
Where the baby I once was has come
to know its own wrinkles once again.
When cars hover and everything is all
shiny, white and smooth.
When what hair I would have is as
silver as space suits.
When my joints ache and my bones
squeak. I'm gonna have an ugly green
sweater with holes in it,
it's gonna be my favorite one too,
the one that I wear on lazy Sunday
afternoons, catching siestas in a
rocking chair on a large porch
somewhere out there
cozily being lulled
to sleep by my own
last breaths...

That day will come.

So today I pretend.
I act as if I was given
a second chance to live.
That I traveled back from
that moment, to right here
and now, to do it all
over again.

## LOVE POEM

if you let it
love will move you
it can dance under the
strobe light of your halo
even if you can't dance

it can enter you
it can mimic water
and seep into every
crack of your being
and quench you

it can cut away the strings

your heart can float
on it like a tiny sailboat
and gently sway on
the waves it creates
and never get lost at sea

with your permission
it can create you

it can reach you
it can heal you

I have witnessed it
with my own foresight
it can tsunami all
of your tears away

all at once for all of forever
I promise you
so I say go forth
and let it

because once inside
it can scrub the soul
completely clean and wash
over the unfinished sand castle
of your dreams giving you
the freedom to rebuild

again

it can rebuild you

and grant you the time to become
whatever it is you wish to become

it has a nourishing quality
it can feed you
it can pour gravy all
over your biscuits
and then some

it can remind you
it can find you

it can rescue you when
you're stranded on the desolate
island of your own heart
you and your volleyball named Wilson

it says that if you open your soul to me
I will open all of my doors for you

and that's what I want

like a game show
I want what's behind
all of her doors
I'll take anything
from a silly $10 blender

to the secrets of the universe

I'll take the giddiness of a first kiss
for the rest of my life
over all of the glitz and splendor
of a winning lottery ticket

so if for any reason at all
you have given up
on yourself
on a relative
on your goals
your ambitions
your childhood fantasies
on biscuits
on love in any of her
endlessly beautiful
shapes and forms

I encourage you to strike a match

and light the bonfire once more
and send your smoke signals into the
heavens and watch in wonderment
as life becomes
a ball of clay in your palm

because if everything anybody
has ever told you about life
is completely wrong

your only hell will be memories
you wished you could've lived
or people you could've loved

so love yourself
and nourish your talents
love your neighbors
no matter what
language they speak
and give all of your pocket change
to all of the people who need it most
because it's the most important thing

see if it means
finding the truth to love to life
I'll search the skies
far and wide, I'll hike the
pyramids or mountains of Mars
in search of a bright dandelion for her

love has been a lamp unto my sandals
it has kept me afloat

and like an old rusted boat anchor
I have this sinking feeling
deep down in my bowels
that when you're drowning

love is keeping your
lungs inflated and your lungs are
keeping your body floating
and to keep the lava flowing
to keep your visions in flight
and find that love is the only
love of your life

all that's required of you
your only responsibility
is to love

## ROCKET FUEL FOR DREAMERS

open as wide as you wish
the furnace of your heart,
of your passion,

and shovel in piles of coal,
take the firewood of your visions,
of your dreams and throw them in,
stoke it with meditation and focus,

and at last drench your heart's wildest
desires with rocket fuel and ignite the
reality you truly seek

## FOURTH DIMENSION

if I were to create the fourth
dimension I would take winter spring
summer and fall and wrap them
around my spine so tightly that my
soul would shoot upward 10x the pull
of gravity and skate across
atmospheres skies and suns the size of
my measureless eyes, you see, the
fourth dimension is where I lay under
cherry blossoms and skip moss
covered thoughts across infinite ponds
that send ripples through my mind
and shatter mirrors above the clouds
staring back at me hands drenched in
acrylics while oils drip from my spirit
I am the breath the bridge from life to
death the in between being that never
rests whose palms flourish with palm
trees and ponders upon a sun that
never sets
I am...

## A CHILDLIKE WONDER

at night
I peek into the mirror
and draw pictures
of stars and moons
where my mouth
and eyes should be
I call it my
higher-self-portrait

I imagine
that my mouth
is a mountain
and that passion
pours out like lava
my shoulders
are the horizon line
my aura the sunrise
rising behind my head
spouting out
like fountain spray
ya see, daydreaming
takes the mist
out of the mystery

at night
I leave my body
I fly my spirit
like Benjamin's kite
like a child full of wonder
lost in a storm

where I become
every folklore & metaphor

and I drift

I am childish
my wish is the same wish
that I have always wished

and that's to lift
a mountain of sand
with puckered fists
pucker my lips
and blow this world a kiss
while its head is hung low
wading in the wattage
and constant glow
of the evening news in hopes
that it will all one day shift
from a great flood
back into a fine mist
high above where kids
play seek & hide
underneath their eyelids
far away from violence

miles above crying sirens
clenching crayons in their fists

at night
I peek beyond the mirror
staring back at me

I dream up new worlds
I color a bright aura
around my body
and draw pictures
of stars and moons
where my mouth
and eyes should be

it makes me feel
closer to home
when the universe
smiles through me like this
because it's home that I miss

I can't imagine a place I'd
rather be more than now
than looking down
on a planet full of lights
some dimming and waning
others are wild flames

all of them lit up
with fire in their gut
in their pit
smoke billowing from nostrils
drooling dragon spit
a bunch of aimless angels
idling along their way
dragging their
blackened heels
over hot coals
it's too hot here

so at night
my cape licks the wind and
I fly into other worlds
that I've created
leaving a trail of crushed crayons
and stardust in my midst
your side of the mirror

my eyes turn lightning white

I moon walk and I rain dance
I pray and I chant with the gods
I shape shift and
move objects with thought
I levitate with light
shooting down from my palms
walking on water
spitting lava like
Pele the island goddess

here, I am ten feet tall and
my talents are super powers
music is language
art is greater than nuclear waste
it's a world I've created
where being human had met
its fate and so turned to dust
hence the mountains we should
be moving with faith to build
a better world for all of us

worlds away from

thunder gods and their flames

cause at night
my cape licks the wind
and I fly high above
the ivory clouds
I time travel lifetimes
ahead of tribal dreamers far out
and listen back for their whispers
and I want them to say
that I had mystical visions

I want storytellers to sit
around their village fire
and speak of me as
if I were a myth

a feathery gift

for them to say
that I was great
a space angel
a water walker
from deep space
that my face was
moon mouthed and starlit
the most beautiful constellation
to come down and visit this place

and fill the world with
miracles and wonder

at night
my head hits the pillow
and scatters into a fine ambiance
painting the world of my imagination

where my crayons become wands
where language becomes song
and I am just child

## EPITOME OF IMPOSSIBLE

back in high school I used to ride the
city bus home, and on that city bus
there were posters perfectly placed in
view with statistics similar to bets on
what my odds were for escaping
poverty:

I am the product of a drug addicted
mother and a fatherless home

a statistical problem

a government-cheese-eating black
teenage fatherless father with cornrow
braided hair and a thousand yard
stare gazing out of another one of
America's hard-knock projects

I'm dead weight on society

they say that the only way out of this
slum that I'm in is self-medication
to numb myself and avoid sobriety

their solution is discourage and to get
rid of me, the problem

I am the epitome of impossible

I shouldn't be here, the posters on the
city bus say so, they say that black
kids my age that have a baby on the
way will most likely grow up to
commit crimes and live in poverty,
they say that I probably won't make it
to see 25 years old anyway

they're telling me to give up today

these posters created by educated men
who have never lived where I have
lived are telling me that I don't have a
snowball's chance in hell to live the
way that they live

they say that it's improbable

they're telling me that the odds are
stacked high against me and that I
should forget about wishing on a star
that I'm a hopeless fallen comet that
hit the earth's atmosphere for
reaching too far that I'll burst and
shatter into a bunch of statistical facts
and figures that don't really even
matter

they're telling me not to try

they're telling me that poor little black
kids will create poor little black kids

and abandon those poor little black
kids and those poor little black kids
will do the same
they build "Planned Parenthoods" in
my hood to prevent this game

it's violent.
they say that it's cyclic that these
social sciences can measure the course
of all human behavior — they think
their kooky little statistics make them
psychic

my anger is ignited
the part of me that believes they're
right doesn't know whether to try or
give up and die

but maybe they don't have it all
figured out; maybe their problem
solving ability is limited to just getting
rid of the problem rather than to
introducing new variables like hope
that could possibly solve them

I'm trying to reason with monsters

the real problem is: their analysis and
interpretation of observed data of one
number measured against another
number in a new unit of time is all

dandy, good and may serve them fine
but

I'm a true rise in their crooked line
the epitome of impossible

yeah
I'm a true rise in their crooked line
because what they couldn't calculate is
the incredible random power of the
human soul on fire

they have no idea how to graph a soul
on ice so now they're scrambling
trying to box up and chalk up a soul
that learned how to glow even when
shrouded in the starkest of nights

impossible

that this poor little black kid could
spring so many traps and understand
that his value is much higher then
what the experts led him to believe

a true rise in their crooked line
I am the epitome of impossible
from what they told me I shouldn't be
here, so one of us is obviously lying
cause pressure makes diamonds and

I am possible

## THE NINJA TURTLE POEM

once upon a time
while fighting my way
out of the gutter
it dawned on me
that everything I ever
needed to know in life
about being a man I learned
from Leonardo, Donatello,
Raphael and Michelangelo.

The Teenage Mutant Ninja Turtles

I learned basic things
like just because your skin
is a different color or
you come from the gutter
doesn't mean that you have
to keep your abilities or
confidence undercover
and where you're raised
or where you're from has
absolutely nothing to do
with who you are becoming
and everything to do with
the superhuman strength
that you possess to overcome it
you've got to overcome it!

and April O'Neil in her
bright yellow jump suit

taught me that we have
the power to change
the evening news, and
strip it of all its darkness
and blues, half truths

and whole lies

I also learned that Shredder
and his cutting cutlery,
his Foot Clan, his
Bebops and Rocksteadys
are hiding everywhere in disguises
like wolves in sheep's clothing
with plans to derail your plans
and slowly pull the wool
over your eyes so stay wise
because their traps are plenty

but the most important lesson
that I learned from 4 mutants
and a noble Rat is that a real man
stays in combat and raises
his children up so that
they don't go out into the world
and re-animate the life they
are so heroically fighting to escape

you don't need guns
you don't even really need capes
You just need to fill a few homes with
fathers

enter Master Splinter my first Mentor

he was everything I never had
and all that I wanted to be
he is the only father I knew
and back then I never realized
that I was gathering all the truth
that this animated rat gave me
what he taught stayed and by 9th
grade...

Splinter came to life and manifested
as my math teacher, Mr. Chapin. No
doubt about it he truly cared and
that's what saved me.

ya see, back in 4th grade at
4 o'clock-Ninja-star sharp
everyday my imagination
was completely free to ooze
underneath dank New York City
streets on FOX TV. I was a fiend.
I had everything from the
T-shirts and action figures to the
video games and trapper keepers.
my mother did her best.
But truth be told trying to raise
a bunch of teenage mutants on
your own in a fatherless home
is a wreck plain and simple

boys need fathers in order

to become men

it's awful when we pretend.
when we're left to fend for
ourselves we begin to mimic
the synthetic polymer over
polished toys in cheap plastic
packaging it's far too easy
for us young bucks
to get the villains and
hero's roles mixed up
and so transform into one
hell of a bastard.

abandon your child?
only a shell of a man
would do something that dastardly!

so if you're in the gutter
in the sewer fighting
to make things right
then do what's right
and stay in the fight

because the world needs its heroes
and the children need their fathers
and now that I'm grown
with a child of my own

I am giving my son everything!
everything I ever wanted!

everything I ever needed and never
had and that's a mutant boy
that became a deadbeat teenage father
and then somehow someway
turned it all around and
miraculously mutated into a Dad

## CONFLICT

I'd like to propose a toast…

to dreams
and to the bold
Men and Women
that dare to dream them
to the wild-eyed visionaries
that plant seeds in their
hearts with hopes
to one day see them
come to pass

for prayers
sweeter than papayas
that rise from the
deepest darkest
depths of our cellars
where my heart
is pumping out
prayers like mass

to the foresight
that illuminates our
foreshadows that
whirl in the glass
of our souls
to those robust
farm workers clad
in jeans, flannels
handkerchiefs and hats

for all the mamas and papas that
wear their skin like worn leather
who are wrinkled and red like raisins
and whose wrinkles hold stories like
wine jugs and whose woes
are ten miles deeper than any
winemaker's pocket book

this one's for them

for all of the grandmas
and grandpas that look like stucco
whose eyes look like ice wines
with frost outlining their irises
for the crows-feet perched
perfectly on their eyelids
and their white hair flowing
like broken clouds passing
through windmill slices
for century old spines like gnarly
vines in vineyards for lilac diamonds
to the god-like elders
for our aging wines and
            their timeless guidance

this one's for floral notes
sung by the brown folks
for the flower vendor
the one that puts
the rose in rosary
for a gorgeous culture
that rose from dirt so openly

for arms that open like blossoms
for womb-like palms that deliver
the grape from bondage
and carry it from
conception to fruition
and beyond the goblet
for the seed that dreams itself
larger than grapes and transcends
wine, song, couplet and sonnet

to cherry pickers like
rebels with barreled chests
waging war with their wages
who hurl their dreams
like Molotov cocktails
into our amber waves of grain
whose knuckles are
gnarled and strained
for the work of a dreamer
is stainless and honest

for the protagonist, the antithesis, the
subplot and most importantly the
conflict

you see
I know copper-skinned
women and men
that work for pennies

I know mothers that
never feel beaten

machine-like Mothers
that clean hotels by day
sell Avon at night
and work the fields
on the weekends
so this one's for freedom

for children with eyes like plums
whose hair looks like dark chocolate
waterfalls pouring out and catching
the sun

for precious sun-flowers
with green thumbs that
have never been embarrassed
of their hardworking parents
that pick pears and pluck asparagus
this one's for the families that get
scattered for work all across the
Americas

its ugly
I know a girl that was
held for ransom at birth
just beneath the border
by bad men known
as Coyotes who you
gotta pay to smuggle dreams
into this country

its beyond ugly
its heart crushing

so this one's for the underbelly
for the juggling of children over rivers
for dodging dogs & militias
for sliding dreams past
the law writers passing
laws higher than the
barbed wire they're casting
the people they're pruning
and the hopes they're smashing

to the Mighty Migrant Worker
may your hands and spine
always nurture the vine
may the cups of all your tomorrows
be filled with the fruits of your labor
and may the dreams you
dream of find freedom
in the land of your neighbor

to you

## CONFLICTO

Quisiera hacer un brindis...

un brindis por los sueños
y por los valientes hombres
y las fuertes mujeres
que se atrevan a soñarlos.
Un brindis por los visionarios
cuyos ojos iluminados
siembran semillas en sus corazones
con la esperanza de verlas, algún día,
llegar a florecer.

Un brindis por los rezos
más dulces que papayas
que se levantan de la más onda
y oscura profundidad
de nuestra bodega
donde mi corazón bombea
los rezos como en la misa.
Y brindemos por la previsión
que ilumina nuestro presagio
que gira en la copa de nuestra alma.

Brindemos por los robustos granjeros
con sus franelas, vaqueros, pañuelos y
gorras por las mamás y los papás
que llevan su piel como cuero gastado
arrugado y rojo como uvas pasas
cuyas arrugas guardan historias como
jarras de vino

cuyas congojas alcanzan diez millas
más allá de la cartera
de cualquier vinicultor

Este es por ellos

por todas las Abuelas
y por todos los Abuelos
quienes se parecen al estuco
cuyos ojos son como vinos helados
con escarcha rodeada en sus iris.
Este es por las patas de gallo
perfectamente posadas
y su cabello cano volando
como nubes pasando
por las tejadas del molino.
Este es por las columnas
vertebrales, antiguas y nudosas
de las parras del viñedo
como diamantes de lilo
y viejos sabios
por nuestro vino añejo
y su guía eterna

Este es por las notas de Flora
cantada por la gente morena y
por la vendedora de rosas
que echa rosas en el rosario y
por una cultura hermosa
que salió de la tierra tan abierta
Este es por los brazos
que se abren como flores

por las palmas del vientre
que salvan a la uva
de su servidumbre
y la lleva de su concepción
al hecho y más allá de la copa
Este es por la semilla
que sueña en sí misma
más allá de las uvas
y trasciende el vino,
el canto, la copla y el soneto.
Este es por Ella.

Este es por los recogedores de cerezas
rebeldes con pecho de barril
declarando la guerra contra sus
sueldos quienes lanzan sus sueños
como cócteles Molotov
hacia nuestras alas amarillas
de trigo, cuyos nudillos
nudosos y cansados
por el trabajo de un soñador
inoxidable y sincero por el
protagonista, el antitesis,
la trama secundaria y, más
importante, el conflicto

Ya ves
Yo conozco a hombres y a mujeres
de piel de cobre que cobran centimos

Yo conozco a Madres
que nunca se sienten vencidas

Madres de máquina
que limpian hoteles de día y
que venden Avon de noche y
que labran en el campo en los findes
este por la libertad

por los Niños con ojos de ciruela
cuyo cabello es como el chocolate
como cataratas vertiendo agua
y atrapando el sol

por los girasoles preciosos
con manos de jardinero
que nunca han sentido la vergüenza
de sus padres obreros
que recogen las peras
y que arrancan el espárrago
este por las familias dispersas por
toda América en busca de trabajo

Y es feo.
Yo conozco a una chica
que fue secuestrada del parto
justo en la frontera
por hombres malos
conocidos como Coyotes
y a quienes se paga
por contrabandear
sueños a este país

La fealdad del hecho
te agrieta el corazón.

Entonces este es por los invisibles
por el malabarismo de los niños por los
ríos por el escape de los perros y los
paramilitares por el tropiezo de los
sueños por el aprobado del legislado
cuyas leyes sobrepasan
el alambre de púas que pasan
por las personas que podan
y los sueños que quiebran

Al Poderoso Obrero Migrante
que tus manos y espinazo
siempre alimente a la parra,
que las copas de tu mañana
estén llenas de las frutas de tu labor
y que encuentren tus sueños
la libertad en la tierra de tu vecino.

Este es por ti.

Conflict translated by
Kyle K. Black, Ph.D.
Assistant Professor of Spanish
Saint Mary's University of Minnesota
kblack@smumn.edu

## FLOWERS FOR MONKS

there are monks
that believe that
we've all lived
enough lifetimes
within infinity
to have all been each
other's mothers

at some point we have all
nurtured and struggled with
one another in some form
or fashion and that we catch
glimpses of our upbringing
and past together
in our very common
moments of passing
each other
by

a dream that seems almost
unfathomable one that tears
seams in the sky

that seven fathoms deep in
meditation we might
actually discover a golden
thread lacing our spirits
a mirror facing a mirror
you and I
united

when she cries I cry

me and my mother
though we drove through life
at night with no headlights
she absolutely brightened
my whole world unfastened
my inner light illuminating
my being bright and whole
and I swear it, I promise
to God she's holy

my mother
her whole being is light
glowing from head to toe
she is a lotus unfolding
with white petals
whirling up and out of
her soul past roots
soil & mulching
a wild blossom rolling
on an open road and
I am simply a branch of
her growing
she's a beautiful rose with
thorns showing
donning a bright white
gown flowing & floating
a few inches above ground
from limb to stem
she's rosy

we drove past
pink flowers popping out
betwixt the pricks of cacti
and pasted plush & pretty
powder blue carnations
on the skyline
passed the pansies
peeling out over
cracked pots and
flower bulbs with
roots in knots
the pride of
a rare orchid family

my mother
she has eyes like heaven's windows
like hallways that lead into forever
like stairwells that climb higher than
ten lighthouses stacked taller than
two gods standing on top of each
others shoulders on tippy toes
giants shrink in her shadow
her halo is a bouquet of sunflowers
she speaks and her wind moves
the clouds looming around me
in fact she lassos a freckled moon
for my imagination to use on the
canvas of coloring books where
back in my childhood
I was often subdued and
mostly consumed by wonder

my mother
I saw her push away the thunder
I saw her draw in the entire
atmosphere and blow away all the
clouds I saw her soak up all my rain
by dragging her gown all
for her sun to rise and come out
once again
she is a cluster of stars
disguised as bone and skin
a purple bell flower ringing in the
wind a true gypsy with a true story to
tell made possible by wanderlust that
began with a kiss
the incredible adventures of
a mother and her three kids

my mother
she's a beautiful night rider
a gorgeous kite flyer
with a heart the size of
a planet in motion
enveloping me
womb-like from birth
to spiritual infancy
forever young in infinity
a candle wick in search of
a dancing intensity
a flame that gently
dazzles within me
cupping me in her
arms like a calla lily

when my glow was empty

my mother would slowly
rock me to sleep
cradle me lovingly
her long flowing hair
softly brushing my cheek
whispering even softer
now there there be meek

although we drove through life
at night with no headlights
with enough fuel to fill
a parking lot full of cars
enough rain to fill
a desert full of tears
enough tears to fill
a monk full of prayers
a heart full of beats
and bumps to pump
enough healing back
into my scars and
life back into her years
she absolutely brightens
my whole entire world, unfastens
my inner light illuminating
my being bright and whole
and I swear it I promise
to God she's holy

## HAIKU FOR MOM

Your ink flows through me.
Thanks for the wonderful gift.
Plans to save the world.

## ENGINES OR BODIES OR WINGS

Those who are not dreaming of waking will remain sleeping in their daydreams and without engines or bodies or wings I'll be riding on a wavelength of awakening aviating in my conscious leap.

## THE DRUNKEN SUFI

when I talk about wine
I talk about exploring
the unknown or my
own ignorance and I'm
ok with being oblivious

I'm ok with looking
slightly foolish and
asking the winemaker
questions like
"what other fruits did you
ferment with these grapes?
or "just how much cinnamon
did you decide to put in this?"
"what do you mean by *vintage*?"

see, Rumi the great Persian
poet once said to
"sell your cleverness and
purchase bewilderment."

to dump your pockets filled
to the seams with Rupees
and let go of the dazzling show
of life and surrender to its beauty

that it's better to be awestruck
then all knowing it's better to
get lost in the mystery of life
and take all that you think

you know and cast it aside
and become a castaway
shipwrecked on the shores
of the sublime and allow the
tide to softly carry you in

clinging to the wreckage is
quite possibly the only sin
that you can commit

so get lost and exhausted
and sprawl yourself out on the
golden shores of a new world
pawn your intellect and
gather up all your wreckage
and whatever's left of your
treasure chests and invest
in the staggering stock
of the uncharted waters
of self

because the real wealth isn't
found in deep pockets
or expensive wines or in
all the Queen's diamonds
it's found in the fat of
looking towards the future,
in the richness of adventure,
and in the kindling of romance,
and all that can lend itself
to pulse and make the heart beat

wine is a world that
I do not know one that
the sea-green waves of
chance gracefully washed me
in on one day a treasure island
so to speak replete with rubies
and emeralds and all the
glimmering jewels
you'd ever want to keep

but the real wealth isn't
found in deep pockets
or expensive wines or in
all the Queen's diamonds
it's found in the fat of
looking towards the future,
in the richness of adventure,
and in the kindling of romance,
it's found in the electricity
that gives birth to pulse
then sends shock waves
throughout your spirit
electrifying the whole being
and gives the heart its beat

when I talk about wine
I talk about letting go
of the safe harbor and
cutting the bowlines free

I talk about tossing
your compass overboard

and letting the calm cool
breath of the gods fill your
sails and boldly steer
you out to sea and finally
discovering that your very
own floating soul is the
only vessel you seek

they called Rumi The Drunken Sufi
because of his love of dancing
he believed that all the beauty
that we perceive to be out there is
actually in here, inside of us, that we
mirror life in precious layers

that the stars are merely chandeliers
catching the light reflecting our spirits
so we have no right not to be bold
we are obligated to out whirl and
out dance the tornadoes that baffle us,
cause we are the chalices of which
the fine wines of life are poured into

so when I talk about wine
I'm talking about us

## LETTER TO LIAM

Dear Liam,

upon receiving the
news of your death
I drove to your parents' house
I sped as fast as I could
as fast as a heavy foot
and trembling hands and
blurred eyes could carry me

I threaded traffic carelessly
radio blaring and clouds bouncing
off the windshield glare
I was buried in sorrow

I felt hollow as though
I had lost all of my leaves

my branches shrank skinny
my eyes looked empty
tears clustered on my
eyelashes like grapes
slipping from vines

harvest had arrived
but I was too weak to
carry her wooden crates

holy fruit in worldly coffins

I arrived at your house
with a cheap bouquet of
flowers in hand somehow

I don't remember buying them

I don't even remember falling
into your parents' arms quivering
and hyperventilating chanting
your name as a divine hymn

the room fell silent

for a moment
I dreamt that you were a
lit candle with endless wax
lighting up the night sky forever

I dreamt that you were tucked
between the wings of angels
and those angels would swoop
through the vineyards and
gently sew you back together

that they would take all of
your beautiful tannins
your ash, your leather
your bitter but brilliant feathers
and softly sew you back together
forever for us

for the suffering

for the sulfur swimming in the
back of my throat and across my
palate

for your parents' sobbing ripe clusters
of tears in the kitchen, into their wine
glasses, in the very moment I was
dreaming of angels, our tears were
pelting the copper colored linoleum
and all of our shoulders were wet with
wine

your mother is beautiful
she looked younger than
I remembered and lighter too
her red hair and white aura
still cast a pinkish glow,
you should see it,
it illuminates the garden

your father, The Balthazar, started
a bottle of '06 Walter Clore Private
Reserve, in minutes it was polished

and for hours we thumbed through
old pictures, shared your stories,
your defeats and glories,

I wondered how many
Northwest Trains and brick walls
bared your name in Krylon paint

I wondered how many hearts
were still wearing your graffiti

I kept waiting for you to come out
of your room how you used to

your blue jeans slightly
sagging over your hip,
a thrift store button-up
draped crookedly over
your torso, your backpack
slung over your shoulder

a heart full of notebooks,
full of rhymes,
full of all kinds of "I'm gonnas"
but there was only an empty hum
ghostly rolling out from the vents.

the suspense was sickening

but you're still here
your music, your letters,
your poems and your paint
are all still here just as you left them
as though you had never left

Liam you were loved
you are still loved and
you will forever be loved

I keep your letters in my glove box,

the needle on the record,
and your name is still in
heavy rotation in my new circles

the Wine Angels have scattered
you over the terrain of memory,
and every now and again, every
so often a lush new story comes
blossoming forward and
brings you back to life.

Your friend,
Jordan

## I CRIED

It's that one of a kind
uncontrollable crying spell

it's that certain moment
when a certain song
plays those certain chords
in that agonizing way kind of cry

almost like your ghost is being
snake-charmed or drawn
right out of your skin against your will
slipping through your bones
gripping your heart strings
with all of its might like
all of your memories
that you tried so hard
to outrun and hide from
all cornered you all at once
then left you in a pit to die
kind of cry

so with a splash of Atlantis
in my sunken eye
the other day
when nobody was watching
when I knew
I was absolutely alone

I cried

I mean I really
opened up and wept
big baby tears leapt
from my lashes
I let it all out
and let all of
yesterday's ashes
blow away

first a cloud formed
then a storm
then a monsoon ensued
and capsized my pontoon
too then a flood
then the ceiling caved in and
all the buckets and
pots filled up
I was completely imbued

it felt good too
it was cleansing
like taking a bath
the salt exalted me

Shakespeare speared it
when he said
"to weep is to make less
the depth of grief."

and that day the clouds
found me under defeat
wading in an indigo water world

with tears up to my teeth
and bleeding ink!

I cried until the whites of my eyes
were reddish pink

my eyes were islands
they were twin waterfalls
rushing in soft silence
like crystal-eyed angels
were dying to slip and slide
from the wet roofs of my eyelids
and leap from clouds
where sunbeams are arrows
shooting out through saline
creating bright rainbows
in the wondrous hereafter
where tears are painfully aching
to be windblown
by one's own laughter

I cried
all day long
at sunrise a somber song
a moistened yawn
a pond at dawn
memories like
bright koi fish
swam boisterously
up my waterfall as
I fell upon the
morning lawn

like dew

they grew and they grew
rambunctious & unruly
a typhoon at high noon
from within my saloon
the wild west tears shot out
my heart was as wide and empty as
15 paces between two gunslingers
squeezing water pistols
as I paced about

and by nightfall all I could see was
aquamarine streams cascading from
night dreams that I was dreaming

I couldn't sleep so I cried
late into the evening
gritting my teeth
then buried my head so deep
into my pillow feathers
flew from my ears
I hid my eyes and my fears
deep in the cotton

I cried as much as I
possibly could that day

in fact I became the ocean
I sobbed seahorses and starfish
I wailed with the whales
I wept so much I made Poseidon blush

my chest opened like the ocean
and the whirlpools swallowed
all of my secret slave ships up
and it freed me!

howling so deeply; it was a prayer.

gargantuan God-like tears
the size of globes
free-fell from my third eye
and on my knees
I thanked God that
I met an angel
just as wet as me
so that we can both fly
into the cool white pools of our irises
where deep visions are nearsighted

that day felt like an eternity
I thought I would never stop crying
but like all my troubles
even this had to pass

then all at once the waves subsided
and I realized that that was it
the tears that I had been crying
that day were so much they floated
me up to the top and out of my pit

## TRAFFIC LIGHTS

as I squint

the streetlights look like stars
stretching across the night sky

and the headlights of cars
look like spinning quasars
the brake lights look like Mars
but rectangular and deformed

the traffic lights are swirling
planets in orbit absorbing
all of everything into blurs

it's cosmic havoc

and I see the universe
reflected in city traffic

## LIGHT

as an offering

I will give you
eons of bouquets of constellations
and the sunray's progeny of
illuminations
vineyards of solar systems
I'll harvest for you

my fetish is feathered
with thoughts of you

the way the sunlight travels
at light speed
ever so lightly

on ether to reach your
incandescent complexion
as soothing winds pass
gently through heavens
through strands of your hair
that's sun-kissed and
softly dressing your divinely
charged aura

and I stare

I stare at things
I know are not there
beautiful things

that are just chimerical carvings
of my mind's imaginings
your love must be maddening

because I detect
dimensions of rhythms
and out of worldly prisms
that send me rising past
the zenith like a phoenix
beyond suns that have fully risen
and you gleam and you glisten

like the reflection of
starlight multiplied by twilight
then magnified 1,000 times
off of the mirror that touches
my soul's vision

it's blinding
brightly lighting
new designs of lightning
inside of my enlightening

it creeps and it seeps
into the depths
where my heart is
encrusted with darkness
and I'm telling you now
if no one else has we all
are truly  starlit beauties

that come without warning

an aesthetic storming warming
every single one of my infinite life's
journeys transforming my yearnings

of old paths I used to seek
I'm dropping the skin now
forever living within now

no longer holding on to
the things I know I could
never keep like precious
jewels or precious loot
or even more precious
above all is the most
precious side of you

I sometimes pursue
into the affluent
treasury of my reveries
in search of a rebirth
that will measure me
timelessly and ever new
and I'll find that when
we are one

enamored with
glamorous light
that is a phantom's kiss
from lantern lips

because
we are all

the products of
stars and suns

we are all
the products of
stars and suns

and you see things
the same way i believe
and i conceive us to be

slivers and shards of the broken glass
of the omni-window that is God's heart

photosynthesis of art
you fill me with light

and I'm high on life
like she be bringing me
bouquets of poetic poppies

I'm like up late at night slinging
kilos of immortal stardust
to the heartless for their catharsis
cause it's marvelous to watch life
without watching our watches

our nature is clock-less

my eyes
slowly skim and skip across
blackened oolong-colored

skies I'm lost when the moon
blows me her silver kisses

I'm drunken with moonshine
inundated with ambience eternally
fermenting in light's chrysalis

it takes discipline and focus to sit
indian-style or full lotus
while flames and smoke
roll and float upwards
from your aura's wholeness

sacrifice and boldness
are the only ways
to break the mold
holding control of your soul
that's carved from the
same substance as light

spaced out! and star struck!
I'm in love with light

## IMMORTAL

I broke the bow

when I drew back
the arrow of my soul

I let go and it flew

forever

## FOREVER WAITING
**(a collaboration with Sarah Watson)**

patience means that
you must deny time
its illusive power
over you

that you should
pretend to be a
golden swan perfectly
perched upon a lotus
in a pond your wings
folded in and riding the
pond's ripples
forever outward

and there you can
rise like the lotuses
endless petals getting
stuck in the air
like tethered clouds
like kites above
the so called
power lines

cause up there
time is sitting still
the sun dial is smiling
at me while her long
shadow stretches with
mine across the skyline

connecting with constellations
and outlining a new path home
eventually

I'm constantly bombarding
the world with my plans,
calendars and clocks, rushing
through traffic MAN

I just can't seem to sit still
my watch watches me tick
I hesitate to meditate
even though I am
desperate to self-explore

to draw back the arrow
of my soul break the bow
and let go to fly forever

to throw banana peels
and pop cans in the
gas tank of my DeLorean
to burn rubber in the sky
kicking hourglasses over
on their side peeling out
past the North Star
speeding like Pegasus
pushing the pedal to the
metal all to be born again

I'm waiting on forever
but waiting on forever

is like expecting to arrive
in a place where forever
is supposed to begin and
denying the very real fact
that you are already in it
and it in you
it lives

it lives in those moments
that sit still when you catch
yourself drifting off staring
into nothing seemingly but
that nothing is actually something
that is gently sucking you in
it sorta feels like your
consciousness is crossing
over into another dimension
that you're not really quite
sure ever existed, but it does
it lives... in us

so I am desperate to walk into
myself, into my body's temple
and light the incense and
chant primordial hymns
with a choir of monks, for my
higher self to beam 1000 watts
brighter and levitate even higher
than it once was...

so

I'm strapping NASA's Rockets to the
helix of my spine and winding back
the hands of time so that I can leave
myself clues like fortune cookies
but in the form of papyrus scrolls
or maps giving myself keys to
the locks of these self-made traps

cause up here
I no longer believe in death
its carcass has found itself
at the dinner table of kings

only believers in life shall live
and life has been found wading
in the oceans of my dreams

waiting has never been what
it seems quite possibly a safe
place to heal for those moments
that sit still just so happen
to reveal unto me a door
cracking open and lighting
my way, outlining a new path
home into eternity

and so I wait...

## A NEW WINE

drink and be merry,
our dreams are upon us
the new wine's springing
from yesterday's vines
have grown this far
just to fill our glasses

let your laughter
howl louder then
the high winds
on the high cliffs of
Goose Ridge,
then laugh some more
but even louder
let your laughter
hear that its own
echo is plodding harder
then the horses trotting
through hills in heaven

let the sound of your
spirit keep spreading

it's spring again
and life is sending a message
something like a love letter
in a bottle, it's symbolic
it's pitching and rolling
over green waves
in the ocean

in hopes that
its ink will
reach that moment
when a distant lover
gets to uncork and
unroll its meaning

life is for the gleaning

it's for the taking
for the dreamers and their long
awaited forethoughts
that manifest upon their waking
for the ones that painstakingly
plant their vision in granite
and understand that
this season brings forth
the abundance of your own
seed planting

so turn the music up and
take chances because
a new wine awaits you
and in the distance she dances
in lilacs and lipstick
in starry candle lights and
where love letters have landed,
in a nightgown woven from
the mystic fabrics you were handed

reward is for the romantics
take chances

take shovels to soil

take the new wine
of your own spirit
and fill it with
every honeysuckle
every grape growing
and blossom blossoming
every bee buzzing
on a bud budding
take every dream
of yours that has ever grown
legs and walked over
your way take her
by the hand whisper
into her ear
your master plan

take all of yesterday's
woes and worries
and throw them away
you are just as new
as all that is new today
drink and be merry
be totally and utterly rapt
with the unwrapping of a new you
a new wine ripens within

never attempt
to pour new wine
into an old wine skin

don’t worry about your past
there’s no turning back
and the future is in you
trust me it whirls inside,
drink and be merry
because we will forever be
in the cleavage of where we
have been and where we are going
we are all infants
at rest upon the
breast of eternity
enjoy the ride!

all of us; new wines
dying on the vine

so turn the music up and
take chances because
a new wine awaits you
and in the distance she dances
in lilacs and lipstick
in starry candle lights and
where love letters have landed,
in a nightgown woven from
the mystic fabrics you were handed
reward is for the romantics

so take shovels to dirt
let your spirit keep spreading
and take chances

## APOCALYPSE HAIKU

zombies won't roam streets
Mayans had it all wrong too
the end is not near

## ODE TO GRAPE

I have a crush on you
you beautiful bulbous
berry of the gods
you galaxy of dark blue stars
you plump and precious
bottle of Pinot Noir

I simply adore you

you sometimes gorgeous green thing
drooping a thousand times from
paintings always nude and next to
tulips the Pinot Gris on your two lips
puts the kiss in kismet
it's serendipitous the way
we have come together

mighty migrant workers
are up to their shins in mud
are sweating in the sun
are plucking darkened rubies
all for my tongue
getting paid in pesos
to slave away
for my fair love

you are endless and without edges
a purple pearled necklace
with a cluster of cleavage
dangling beneath it

a scarlet goddess
robed in a red dress
sagging on the vine
marauding my fantasies
every midnight
when the sky light is merlot-like

I love it when you
bat your lashes at me
while layered in lingerie
then splash into my cup
like purple rain and
climax when you pass
my tongue and come
into long stemmed glasses
you look like a pin-up doll
showing off your legs & ass
making my heart patter
fast and then faster
until my pulse is unfastened

alas
you are crimson
a succubus
a full-bodied Jezebel
who has had
everybody's filthy hands on you
from train hopping hobos
to snobs with mountains of
dollar bills you've slept in crates
in dirt fields next to windmills
in alleys next to burning barrels

and even in sheets woven
from the finest of silks

but I don't care about
your cheap past
and how you were
stepped on daily
how your delicate skin
has been beaten and smashed
or when you lived in boxes
with eyes blue & black
to me you are a rose that grew
from history's trash

my love is unconditional

you are both the Mother Teresa
and Mary Magdalene of all the fruits
a noble truth serum with heavenly
roots and sauvignon rivers
flowing bright though your veins
turning tongues into pure silver
a miracle like magic a mystic
once summoned you from
a glass of water
to make men meek
you put the vine in divine
and now my mind is an aimless
cork afloat a placid sea
sacred grape to saintly mate
hallowed be thy taste
Ms. Holy Water if you please

I love you
because when I was sour
when my heart was withering
away like a raisin in the sun
when every part of me shattered
asunder and I was picking up
the pieces all over the streets
you stood by in the countryside
waiting for me to mature
and then cherry-blossomed into my
life singing a song of dreams of
tomorrows and swept all of my
sorrows away

I want you to know that

sitting on the couch with you
is enough for me
we can watch the sun
melt like gold into the hills
we can imagine that the
sun is sinking into the earth
and impregnating her with
our hopes and with our dreams
we can watch as she gives
birth as the harvest
ripens and comes forth
and brings our visions
full circle back into being
and so when we toast we'll know
that our souls are swallowing
their own dreams

## BEYOND THE CRUSH

A red man usually I am
rolling in the sheets with
my scantily-clad petit faithful
smashing grapes between our teeth
in a dream state high above sleep
lost in purple mountains and fruited
plains where desire has me wakeful

though I fell asleep beneath the
flowers

in this case, one day under an
umbrella a sleazy little Riesling came
drizzling by a sweet but dry, apple of
my eye, a fair pear unparalleled with
legs that paired perfectly well with my
goblet cause I'm a grape goblin with
fangs that feast on the fruit of the
flesh so pardon my Kama

I can explain!

I'm losing my marbles darlin'
your legs are two Greek Pillars
climbing high into white heavens,
they flirt with the gods,
you're a green-eyed goddess,
a firecracker scarlet starlet
lipstick on the collar with
bonfire hair and pink and

peach freckles speckled sexily
from head to toe, a sweetheart
that's hard to wallow with...

your legs have walked all the
way from Austria they deserve
an applause and the wine tasters
are surely a flooded audience
I just want to be lost in
the storm of your bra
lost in the vineyard's thralls
with a young fly virgin from
Germany laced from toe to waist
in laces from Alsace
a French maid made to
bathe in a golden lake
for goodness sake she
sparkles with greatness

you could say I'm high
on her winetasting

you don't understand!

your puckered lips, your blown kisses
are a smoking pistil you're a smoking
mistress on Red Mountain holding a
Cuban-rolled stogie smoking beneath
your nose with nylon-legs crossed in
full body language and crisscrossing
your heart, good God your hot!

en fuego, I'll dance the tango with you
Senorita in rain right as golden
sangria! Mama Mia, I need to decant
I'm panting the soul of Italy in my
riddles playing a fiddle skipping along
singing a silver man's song sipping
kerosene from a canteen as this sleazy
little Riesling honey-coats tongue!

give me a chance!

I want to wrap you in a hammock
knap you in the sack and find you
napping softly in the lap of Napa
Valley slowly disrobing to lightning
and thundering rolling in the covers
like Riesling lovers so much so that
I've been labeled a drunk intoxicated
by your loving

I love her lush lashes how they rise up
like Marilyn Monroe's skirt after a
gust of steam blasts the model in a
bottle or the actress I want to sip from
my mattress I'm a maverick after it
and she's a high-maintenance
balancing act that's constantly on my
conscience, noble rot or spoiled brat I
have no other choice but to nickname
you Constance

It's not my fault!

you're smashing, a hoot, I get a kick
out of you a laughing spasm, a grape-
gasm for the grabbing a berry special
double entendre your name a
winemaker's mantra so come fly with
Sinatra

what more can I say?

forgive me…

I'm a Brut
and you're a rare but fair-skinned
Champagne, a high-yellow red-bone
crush so busty and buxom that the
buttons are busting off your
bottle of bubbly, you're a bottle of lust
for the guzzling the loveliest trouble
that's always ripe for the tussling –

could you blame me?

no more excuses!
it's better to stick with the truth
you are simply the cutest fruit to have
ever seduced me

## MOONSHINE

Even with the stars on foot patrol
and the sun rolling surveillance
some how, some way
you've bagged illumination,
you robbed a full moon
for its gentle white glow,
and it shows, like new jewels
in the window on display
your pearly corona splayed.
and good thing you did
nab the night for its day–
it looks much better
sprouted about your
delicate shoulders
and beaming face...

## GODDESS

Truth is
I've got no game
you are divine
a breath of fresh air
to new lungs
a poem in motion
your ink leaping
from every couplet
and sonnet ever written
I'm smitten.
Amber waves flowing
over oceans
between continents
connecting our consciousness
palms full of lotus blossoms
I'm awestruck you're
that awesome
a cosmic Goddess
donning a starlit garland
levitating through an
eternal garden...

## WARRIOR

You're beautiful to me
but I couldn't simply
call you pretty.

Pickup lines
about dimples and shells
are often hollow
and empty

I always fall in
somehow.

Don't be mad at me
just take this as
free music or
poetic flattery

I've been scorched
by the light of my own
enlightenment.

Cashed in love, for ammo.
Lit my stove with
old poems even.

Now we're at war

and

You're a warrior

you are the revolutionary
that I have always wanted
in my circle, on my side.
I gobble your propaganda
up like scarce rations.

My heart beats
like street riots; you smash
my windows and set fire
to my prayer rugs and temples.

Beautifully cruel; spotless.

Your eyelashes are weapons that
bat arrows into my quiet peace.

So colonize me
maraud my huts
loot my throat
for all of its metaphors

You leave me speechless

You're a ripe peach
an orchard's high priestess
you bonfire the trees
just to free your flames
nobody can handle
your sweetness

Though I'm glad you came.

Astral artistry you come
from stars obviously
you're beyond a work of art
polished and carved marble
Mona Lisa be damned
a broken dam
your beauty has
flooded my lands

Once again

The past
has left me scarred
and I know that girls from
the future dig scars
way more than
fancy cars and
here we are.

## SHE'S FLY

she's fly
and not just like slang in '85
she's fly like angel's wings on babies
dangling from clouds in Raphael
Santi's famous painting fly like
Michelangelo's hanging masterpiece
God's creation

and she speaks the language
of eternity with love skinnydipping
from the tip of her tongue she could be
the one I've been waiting for and
possibly the one that I came for

'cause I swear I would harvest every
star from every galaxy for her I would
and if I could I would scribble both of
our names in the moon

and trace them with a heart
together there forever never to be
touched by weather

versus the world that we live in
that seems to be withering away
and falling apart all around us but we
bloom two of a kind working in unison
like one mind

she is my queen
and I am her worker bee
building a honeycomb in her beehive
pollinating patiently 'cause this
worker bee be longing for her inside

and yes
I know that that metaphor could have
been written by a child but the truth
is she makes me smile so my youth is
let loose and running wild, I'm feeling
the way I used to feel so it's
worthwhile

you see, I went from walking on water
to completely drowning

to finally finding someone who keeps
my heart pounding

she glows
she flies

and I don't care why
'cause here in the afterlife
she conquers the heavens soaring
through the skies apparently
transparent blending in with the
horizon or even disguised in
the wings of butterflies
1000 watts brighter than fireflies
a flying angel with bonfires

like burning eyes
into infinity she glides divine
she's levitating in my mind

fly
above the mountains
above the falcons
and beyond the clouds
her aura could cool the sun down
and she gallops through my dreams
never touching ground

haunting me peacefully
it's the most profound feeling
and I just want to be part of her flight
tonight right now I want us to leave
our bodies together and never return
to fly

forever beyond
forever beyond
forever beyond this lifetime

'cause I might have found love this
lifetime I might have finally found
what I came searching for when I
crept into this lifetime and if we fly
away now love could be ours forever

then I could sever my mind
forever from my body
building wings on my soul

to unfurl and leave this world

having never lost love
and having only lost myself in love
with her I am in love with her

I'm in love with her wings
I'm in love with her dreams
and I'm in love with
the dreams she has for me
to fly

## WORKIN' MY WAY UP

your toes are lollipops I swear it, they
beg for thousands of licks, they want
to dissolve onto my tongue, they long
to vanish into a sweet nothing the way
they tip-toe across my sweet tooth

your stilettos are a harem full of toes
something like Egyptian harlots, they
smother me, I'm outnumbered 10 to 1,
I surrender! your calves are shotguns
locked and loaded, they got my
fingerprints all over the trigger
they're double-barreled and I am a
trigger-happy fool, I figure I can get
away with a crime like this

your calves are caramel fondue, a
waterfall of sorts pouring out of short
shorts cascading and parading
beneath thighs

your thighs are maddening they lock
me up in padded rooms they tackle me
and sedate me, I overdose on brain
candy
—they won't let me out no matter how
sane I pretend to be.

my mind is a circus where King Kong
is going bananas pounding his chest

and climbing up them. your thighs are
that bad to be around! your legs are
two bank robbers in fishnet masks,
holding up my bank, sticking up the
joint, bagging all my cash, then
celebrating on the Pacific in Mexico
weeks later in a hotel, popping corks,
spilling champagne all over the place
and all over the sheets too

your legs are a getaway car burning
rubber, a Firebird with a golden
phoenix tattooed to the hood, peeling
out just blocks away from cops, I quit
my job for them: and baby I want
a ride!

you are as bad as they come!

your hips are cliffs that sky divers
seek out, I dive off of them and into
them–
sometimes my chute feels like it may
not open but I take my chances hoping
that you will catch me somehow

your hips look like vintage
bookshelves full of books on Kama
Sutra poses and prose, they've got
metaphor written all over them and
I'm your most studious student a

slightly rude prude but still showing
prudence for your literature

your ass is a sold-out rock concert,
head banger heaven, I smash my
guitar on stage, I kick the drums over,
the mosh pit loses total control but the
show must go on so I stage dive, I
crowd surf into your stonewashed
jeans

your navel is a shot glass, a splash of
tequila, a sake bomb, a pond in the
desert, a mirage, I'm a lost and thirsty
wanderer, lost in wonder at the sight
of your awe

your inny has me hanging out later
than I should I'm worried about work,
I'm drafting lies to tell my boss, but
your belly button presses all the right
buttons and baby doll you are worth it!

your rib cage locked me up and threw
away the key, it's an hourglass and
I'm your prisoner forever, I grip your
ribs and scream for the guards, I rattle
my coffee mug in a clankety-clank
against them, they're unfair, they're a
crooked Shawshank warden extorting
me!

and your breasts, Good God
your breasts are two Buddhist temples
glowing high above the jungle, and
holy cow's milk am I a monk in search
of his higher self, high powered and
divine.

they are hand grenades and I pull the
pin out with my teeth, I am Che ready
to get the revolution started!

they are speakers on a ghetto blaster,
a boom box that makes this hustler's
heart beat, I lose sleep working my
way up and I am working my way up
'cause I just want to be on top!

the pits in your collarbones are
antique teacups at teatime; I could
steep all day inside of them, your neck
is a stripper pole no a lamp post and
at the top an atomic aura blasts the
clothes off my bones…

and if there is anything, anything at
all that I have forgotten, that I've
missed, the next time you see me at
the circus eating cotton candy and
licking my lips, please do me a favor,
blow me away and blow me a kiss!

## PISTOL-WHIPPED

For years I had been
caught in the cross hairs
of your crossed legs; your
navel a barrel pressed
softly against my forehead
at point blank range
me, on my knees
gripping the pearl handle
begging for your sweet life.

## FORTUNE

deep beneath the golden
sands of my flesh
beneath my deserted chest
there has been a
longing in my soul
and that longing
has created pressure
and that pressure has
turned my heart into
a precious stone

the dumb luck of stumbling
upon something rare where
I thought there was nothing
that could be touched but air
you are my everything
and I vow from this day forward
to honor you as such

you are my sustenance
and your words
are my clouds like stairs
that I climb when I feel
that I just can't breathe
without you by my side
my lungs are runaway balloons
in vanishing skies

our eyes sparkle like jewels
like torches lighting up tombs

filled with gold
beneath the sands of my flesh
I'm filled with gold
beneath my skin
my spirit blows breath
against my ribs
like winds to wind chimes
I am filled with your song

and together our spirits sing
to the high heavens times seven
while showered in blessings
from above and beyond

our hearts are brightened
rubies pulsating jewelry
as we walk in unity
your hand in my palm

(forever) like a diamond
you are like a diamond
you shine even when in a dark cave
and 10x brighter when the sun bathes

your love is grand it glows
and the grandeur has captured
my soul from where all of my
abundance flows it's the only
wealth that I care to know
therefore I surrender bones
my indigence and poverty

going forth
I am lighting my home
with nothing more than the
oil of your aura from
your lamp to my lamp
the flame ebbs and flows

so that in the infinite we will be
lit like candlesticks and our wax
will pour endless down our firearms
flowing from our heart's core

I want you to know that
you are adored that you are truly
heaven's blessed ornament
the master's masterpiece

and its worlds beyond
anything like worship
I would battle a warship armed
with nothing more than an ore
for you

there are not enough
treasures in this world that compare
to my wealth emeralds pour out of the
clouds and diamond-filled mountains
don't even begin to amount with
the fortune I have built with you

I'm on wings
it's beyond butterflies

swarming in a whirling
vortex in my stomach
it's complex it's
in my solar plexus
from my silver tongue
to your pearl necklace
my cup runneth over
the whole world over
the spill is measureless

and I only know this
because I only notice
when I'm next to you
what I'm trying to say
is that I treasure you
I do

## TXT MSG FOR HER INSOMNIA

overhead
sheep leap
and kick clouds
so sleep deep my love
tomorrow is wrapped in
today's sheets

## FLY

All of their wind is tangled in the trees
and their breath never seems to take
the shape they want. My tornadoes
are clearing pathways to your hearts.
The chances of us all escaping this
time are greater than they have ever
been…

I say we all hold hands and leap

## ANOTHER GIGANTIC DREAM

it's recurring, my pillow shrinks
to a cotton ball during sleep

and last night I had another
dream that I was a giant

my footprints created ponds
I could even cup the sun in my palms

and my laughter rang out
around the rings of Saturn
I defied science

my clothes were ten times too small
and upon my shoulders I saw
bird's nests and moss covering
my colossal worn cloth

I looked mountainous; cypress.
the tallest trees came
only to my knees

even the statue of liberty
was a pygmy next to me
it was lonely being the only one
this tall but at least I was free

## THE ICARUS ODE

Son,

Remember that time
I said I would fight a
bear for you? I meant
it and this is what
I meant by it...

a father's love is
sometimes grizzly
and hard to describe
so you owe it to both
your life and mine
to climb

I dare you to defy gravity

I dare you to
crane your neck back
outstretch your arms
point your toes towards
the earth and lift off

in fact I double dog no
I triple double dog dare you
to light the rockets idling
on standby in your heart's
chakra and take off flying

I'll even stitch a Nike swoosh

into the side of your aviator cap

I'll scoop cotton clouds out of
the sky by the palm-full with
rocket fuel and stuff them
in your jet pack

I'm here to help you light the fuse.

I'm here to help your rockets
blast off and shoot and
watch the dreams of your
inner space manifest
in your outer space

and to make sure that
the crows that would
try to stop you choke on the
chemtrails you fume the
sky with... all powder blue.

oh the places you'll glow
upward and outward

and this could just be
the big sappy heart of
fatherly love but I know
that you're special
you're truly different
and I can see that
all of their wind is
tangled in the trees

and their breath
never seems to take
the shape they want
but your tornadoes can
clear pathways to their
hearts and free them
'cause the chances of us
all escaping this time
are greater than they
have ever been

I say we hold each other's
hands and leap

and if you begin
to freefall in life
because in life you will
get that sensation that
feeling that no nets
will catch you, that there
are no clouds to claw
no safety lines to cling to
when all of your wax
has melted

your feathers falling in
slow motion all around you
just know that I will
always be here for you

fighting the bears

may you burn so brightly
that any rain cloud would
dissipate in your presence

a force field borne from lessons

'cause we fathers see ourselves
as weathered staircases for
our children to climb to greater
heights—heights that couldn't be
reached without the constant
guidance, the coloring on walls
of heaven or the mapping
out of the skies when tucking
you into bed at night, it's all
for the growth, for the flight,
for the dipping of the arrowheads
of our spirits into the oil of life
to fly forward with courage

Khalil Gibran said that
"We are the bows from which
our children as living arrows
are sent forth."

and to think that when I was
15 years old I cried and begged
your mom to have an abortion

I was scared of course
but now that you're 17
and I look into your

large brown eyes
and I watch your shoulders
begin to widen like mine
I'll admit it, I'm still
just as frightened
as the day that I found
out that I had a living
breathing child alive
inside of that very woman
I cried too
though we don't get
along anymore
I know that she
was a lot wiser
than I, 'cause today
I honestly would be
lost in life without you
every day my heart
swells with pride
I'm so glad you're mine

I'm opening the door
and giving you the keys
to the sky, wax and feathers,
but more importantly
a map to yourself that
you will find

may you fly so high that
the angels have to look up to you
for guidance, that your never
ending story is one filled with

triumph and tails of love
and super human pilots
fighting crime

I read somewhere along
the path that we should
raise our children to be
messiahs.

that we should leave open
the windows of their young
minds in the event of the
night falling to silent
so they can defy gravity
with one wing of the arts
the other wing of sciences

whatever happens from
here on out it'll be me and
you forever and ever and ever
and we've got a whole lab full of
wax and feathers and treasures
plus we're clever so we can fly
forever and ever and ever
if we have to we'll strap
the jetpacks on ourselves
we'll turn and crank the
pulleys and pistons and get them
to spinning in our hearts and
pull the tarps off of our wings,
jumpstart our engines
and oil up our flying parts

that have rusted over
then we will fly... with sheer will
'cause it's never ever ever over
even though sometimes that's
how it may feel, just know that
you will move all the mountains
you please with a gentle
flapping of your wings,
and you will reach higher
states of awareness and being
that I could never reach
'cause you and I—we'll go on
flapping forever, our hearts
pulsing like propellers as
we softly lift off together
father and son escaping gravity
leaping from the tower, and
maybe this way its better...

## YARN HAIKU

We're all just tangled
balls of yarn trying to un-
ravel our way home.

## NOTES ON A TRAIN TO BIG SUR

Amtrak train carts are a string of pop cans hurling themselves gently into fading horizons, outskirts of small towns, untouched dark lush forests and the motherly cradling of train bridges. I see a faint reflection of *me* on the face of the looking glass—I look superimposed on the smear of endless landscapes we pass through. She gently wobbles eastward city-by-city and farm-by-farm, rocking me to sleep; it's womblike.

The staff and even the conductor lack social skills. I pretend that I'm talking to stones and moss that have no idea what it's like to be bursting with stars. They have no idea that they are just giants tied down by spider webs. I imagine that they have been lulled into a sleepy zombie-like trance by the constant motion, the constant coming and going in straight circles, never arriving at any real destination, long faces jailed in by wrinkles, and bloodshot eyes that hold no glare. I pray that my bonfire grows violently forever but stays soft and approachable as a newborn's drool-filled cheek.

…and the passing streetlights are large guardian statues holding torches high above the train. Behind us they blend in with the setting constellations. They are stars wired together blowing one another kisses, serenading the night clouds and casting their ghostly neck-like shadows on billowing engine smoke.

Ten hours later we all wake up and yawn in symphony—the whole choir. Retired train carts covered from toe to skull in rust surround us. Some of them have graffiti on them from the 1980s—they are ancient tombs with eroding hieroglyphics. There are indecipherable messages smeared in the corner of my eye. Stray dogs and scrap metal are ornaments here. The only treasure to be had is the leaving of stones unturned and filling your pockets with the jewels of wonder. Besides, the transients and the hounds have pissed on everything; everything is now rust; even the sun averts its wild blazing eye. Not even the vines will touch these sad carts. The train is a needle threading its way through a hobo's lean-to, the gathering grounds of stray dogs and cats, and the sinking sun bobbing and throbbing on the skyline. I'm aggravated that we've stopped. I miss the motion. And to top it all off, the woman wearing coke bottles next to me won't shut the hell up about her damn cat! But she's sweet and anxious to get home, so I listen genuinely. Perfect strangers like her are all too common and her simple joy is not so common these days.

Five hours past Portland there are fields filled with sheep. A new cast of travelers have filled the seats all around me. The guy next to me moved to find cushy seating—all of the new strangers are in the same mood: zombie. It eats your heart out to think that humanity is asleep with clipped wings.

There's a circle of trees a mile from our train. They're holding hands and bowing their heads as if in prayer. It's spiritual. I'm starting to get the feeling that my soul is shedding its skin again. I have dove into fires like this before—on the road—Greyhound busses from coast to coast, station wagon with mom across country when I was a kid, falling into depressions and clawing my way back out. I have lived all varieties of the phoenix bird. It's been spiritual; it always is spiritual for me.

The train jerks to a stop right outside of a prison. A dozen or so glossy-eyed passengers are smoking and tossing small talk back and forth like spare change. We can see inmates in the windows, we're all staring at each other. We're curious about the stories behind what they did; they just want to know where we're going. Our hearts are poker hands that we will never get to see.

My gods, the night is falling fast, the stars, they look like candlelit lanterns softly parachuting to earth. Half of the train is drunk; the other half of us are intoxicated from the scenery. Mountains like breasts of goddesses, pink clouds swallowed by blackness. The whole train trembles as we push through ecstasy. I've never traveled like this before, where angels can peel the ether back like curtains and spy on my highest fantasies.

After ten hours on a train with strangers, well, the strange evaporates and you see yourself in them, someone that has been waiting to break the silence. Now fifteen hours away from destiny, perfect strangers are milking the moon of its entire glow.

Palm trees in the fall are like a drunk relative wearing a Hawaiian shirt at a funeral, unless you're here. We're limping along littered tracks in San Jose, through smog-filled sky; the sun looks like a soft peach shedding its fuzz over the distant hills. Everything close to the train, the businesses and the neighborhoods, are the filthiest you've ever seen, but just a few peeks above the city-top beauty reigns supreme as far as you can see.

I'm getting closer. On a shuttle to Monterey there's a group of French tourists bickering with the driver about "smoke, a smoke break." She is ignoring them by telling me about all of the glory and majesty of Big Sur. The French tourists are curling their lips and talking about "rude Americans," the driver quips back with "rude French people." I can't help but laugh and then I am immediately absorbed into the yellow blue and pink clouds hovering over the ocean.

There are some experiences and environments so divinely rare that trying to put words to them would be as futile as trying to explain the theory of relativity to a fruit fly—it would nag you mad! My few days spent at Big Sur were beyond poetry, beyond words, and if trying to describe it to people sent you into a manic state, the beauty and intelligence that you have soaked in from the utopia would undoubtedly rescue you from the badlands of your psyche upon your humble request. It's God's Mona Lisa. See, what an awful description that was; my own metaphor betrays me.

When a 20-year-old girl on a train
asks a 22-year-old guy
"How old do I look?"
What she's really asking is am I pretty enough to be loved or made love to. But what she's saying is can you love me the way my father couldn't, could you carry me when my arms are full of my own tears, can you heal my wounds, please, I will give you my outsides if you care for my insides, I'll give you all my flesh just to hear you fake the words *I love you*. The two are in for a counterfeit trade. She'll fake

orgasms with real tenderness. And he will fake love for it. The joy will fade into a blur like the scenery we're speeding past. We want to hold on to the sun melting into a wavy puddle on the lake, but its impossible. It sinks and gets washed up on the memory banks like a muddy waterlogged boot missing its other half. Love is a moving target, it requires a constant chasing, more and more logs if the bonfire is going to be wild. She's dead inside and she sees sex as the only living thing she has to offer him, like a bright flower resting on a tomb in a graveyard. She's a wandering ghost waiting to ascend. And he, he's got nowhere to go, so why not.

Sy Safransky is the leader of the retreat I'm heading to in Big Sur. He created *The Sun Magazine* thirty years ago. They recently advertised a contest to win an all-expense-paid writing retreat. They chose two people to go the Esalen Institute in Big Sur, CA. I was a lucky winner!

Right now, on the train, I am sitting near three burly fellas wearing dirty cover-alls and they've got more scruff than Vikings. Behind them there are two ladies in their early thirties holding a baby. The two ladies are complaining to all of the passengers about the "rude inconsiderate idiot staff and asshole conductor, they're like talking to freakin' rocks I swear!" The baby is hunched over the back of the seat with a gigantic smile, gleaming with drool. The three men can't see it but they have childhood smeared all over their faces. They are just as giddy and happy as the baby that they can't seem to pry their eyes off of. Sy, when reading notes from his notebook yesterday morning at the retreat, said, "Babies make us feel beautiful when we're in their presence." The obnoxious train is filled with baby light right now; it's beautiful. The baby's name is Scarlet, but there's nothing more pure than her on this train.

Jordan Chaney
10-24-2011

# GLOSSARY

Words defined in order of appearance.

## TIME MACHINE

**Finite** –Limit; an end
**Hover** –To float
**Siesta** –A short nap
**Cozily** –Comfortably
**Lulled** –To soothe; quiet

## LOVE POEM

**Strobe Light** –An electronic light that flashes; Often found at celebrations or dances
**Halo** –A circle of light found above and around the head of a saint or person of divinity
**Mimic** –To imitate or resemble
**Seep** –To flow or leak
**Quench** –To satisfy by drinking
**Foresight** –An ability that allows one to predict the possible outcomes of the future
**Tsunami** –Natural disaster, A high sea wave caused by an earthquake
**Nourish** –To provide necessary substances for good health such as food and water

**Volleyball Named Wilson** – Reference from the movie *Castaway* starring Tom Hanks. In the movie Tom Hank's character becomes so lonely that he forms a friendship with a volleyball that washed ashore with him

**Glitz** –A glamorous, superficial display

**Splendor** –A magnificent and grand appearance

**Ambitions** –One's desires and visions to achieve something in life

**Bonfire** –A large fire built outdoors

**Smoke Signals** –smoke columns used in patterns to create a message to someone

**Dandelion** –A bright yellow flower with a globular head

## ROCKET FUEL FOR DREAMERS

**Furnace** –A structure similar to an oven sometimes fired by gas oil or wood used as a heating system

**Passion** –A strong almost uncontrollable emotion; An intense desire about or for something

**Meditation** –A state of intense focus. A practice of holy people or monks; One of the doors to enlightenment or total awareness of self

**Rocket Fuel** –Fuel that is used to shoot rockets into space; Motivation, Passion, Personal Power

## FOURTH DIMENSION

**Dimension** –Another realm not detected by plain sight.
**Gravity** –A force that attracts all bodies or masses to the center of the earth.
**Atmosphere** –The air in any place, the space surrounding and enveloping earth or other planets.
**Acrylics and Oils** – Paints used to create works of art on canvass and other surfaces.

## A CHILD-LIKE WONDER

**Higher Self** –The spiritual self, the true self; soul
**Horizon** –The skyline where the earth surface and the sky appear to blend into one another
**Aura** –The soul; the light around the heads of saints
**Spouting** –Water flowing out from a point, fountain-like
**Folklore** –Traditional beliefs and stories of a community, usually passed

down through spoken word and word of mouth

**Metaphor** –Used in poetry and other writings; A figure of speech where one idea is applied to an object or action of another idea to illustrate a point

**Dimming** –A light fading in brightness

**Waning** –To decrease in power, to become weaker

**Billowing** –A swell of some sort; smoke rolling out of a window of a burning building; outward and upward

**Idling** –Not in use; on standby, no motion

**Moonwalk** –Popular dance created in the 1980s by the late Michael Jackson

**Rain Dance** –A ritualistic dance done to summon rain

**Pele** –Hawaiian religion; the goddess of fire

**Thunder Gods** –A metaphor describing religions that use fear and intimidation to gain compliance from their followers

**Mystical** –Spiritual, religious, supernatural

**Myth** –Folk tale, story, legend.

**Water Walker** –One of the abilities of Jesus Christ

**Constellation** –A formation made up of stars forming some kind of mythological figure
**Miracles** –An unexplainable act or situation that defies science and the natural world
**Ambiance** –The character, feeling or personality of a place
**Wands** –A thin stick or rod possessing some sort of magical power

## EPITOME OF IMPOSSIBLE

**Statistics** –The science of collecting and analyzing data in large quantities
**Poverty** –The state of being poor
**Projects** –The ghetto
**Sobriety** – The state of being sober
**Epitome** – The perfect example of something
**Improbable** –Unlikely
**Comet** –A celestial object made up of dust and ice
**Cyclic** –Something that happens in cycles
**Kooky** –Crazy
**Psychic** –Telepathy or clairvoyance
**Hope** –A trust or expectation that something that you want to happen will in fact happen despite the apparent odds

**Analysis** –To examine something closely
**Dandy** –Excellent
**Shrouded** –Covered, cloaked
**Stark** –Sharply defined, clear

## THE NINJA TURTLE POEM

**Gutter** –Ghetto, drain, sewer
**Dawn** –Daybreak
**Leonardo, Donatello, Raphael, Michelangelo** –The four great renaissance painters of the hit cartoon Teenage Mutant Ninja Turtles
**April O'Neil** –The News Reporter
**Shredder** –The Evil Villain
**Cutlery** –Cutting utensils
**Foot Clan** –Shredder's army
**Bebops and Rocksteadys** –Shredder's minions, henchmen
**Re-animate** –Revive; bring back to life
**Master Splinter** –The father or mentor of the Ninja Turtles
**Mentor** –Guide, teacher, guru, counselor
**Manifested** –Reveal, show, display
**Ooze** –Seep, flow, trickle. Also, the green radioactive ooze that apparently transformed the Ninja Turtles into who they are
**Dank** –Damp

**Fiend** –A person extremely infatuated with something
**Mimic** –Copy, imitate
**Synthetic Polymer** –Plastic
**Villains** –The bad guys. Criminals
**Bastard** –A child born out of wedlock
**Dastardly** –Wicked
**Mutant** –Freak, monster

## CONFLICT

**Visionaries** –A person who thinks about and plans the future; a seer
**Papayas** –Tropical fruits, melons
**Cellars** –Rooms below ground to store wine
**Mass** –Holy Communion, Catholic worship
**Foresight** –The ability to predict the future
**Illuminates** –Lights up
**Foreshadows** –Warns of future events
**Robust** –Healthy, strong, vigorous
**Clad** –Clothed in
**Stucco** –Plaster used for coating architectural surfaces for decoration
**Irises** –The colored part of the eye
**Crow's-feet** –The hairline wrinkles near the outer sides of the eyes
**Perched** –A place where a bird has rested or sat, like a branch

**Gnarly** –Unattractive, rugged
**Lilac** –A pale pinkish color
**Vendor** –A trader in the street
**Rosary** –A string of beads for keeping count of devotion
**Bondage** –Being a slave
**Goblet** –A drinking glass with a bowl-shape to it
**Couplet** –Two lines of verse, usually in the same meter, joined by rhyme
**Sonnet** –A poem of 14 lines using formal rhyme schemes
**Molotov Cocktail** –A crude bomb made out of a vodka bottle and a fuse made from a cloth
**Gnarled** –Rough and twisted
**Protagonist** –The hero, the leading role in any story
**Antithesis** –A person that is the direct opposite of another person
**Subplot** –A side plot in a story
**Green Thumb** –One's natural ability to grow plants
**Underbelly** –The soft white underside of an animal
**Militia** –A military force of able-bodied citizens
**Pruning** –To trim a shrub or bush

## FLOWERS FOR MONKS

**Infinity** –Forever
**Unfathomable** –Unthinkable, unimaginable
**Fathoms** –A measurement of depth
**Lotus** –A large white lily
**Mulching** –Decayed bark, leaves and other types of compost
**Donning** –Wearing clothing
**Betwixt** –Between
**Cacti** –Plural for cactus
**Carnations, Pansies, Orchids**–Flowers
**Lassos** –Ropes
**Subdued** –Quiet, depressed
**Gypsy** –Traveling person, a free-spirited person
**Wanderlust** –A person that has a strong passion to travel to various places
**Calla lily** –A cupped flower
**Meek** –Gentle, honest, humble

## THE DRUNKEN SUFI

**Sufi** –A Muslim Mystic
**Ferment** –Brew. Give rise to
**Vintage** –High-quality, superior
**Rumi** –A 13th Century Persian Poet
**Cleverness** –Intelligence, brightness, smarts

**Bewilderment** –Confusion
**Rupees** –The monetary unit of several Middle Eastern regions
**Awestruck** –To be filled with awe Amazed
**Sublime** –Beauty and great admiration
**Sprawl** –To stretch out
**Pawn** –Put in pawn, used as collateral on a loan
**Uncharted** –Unmapped
**Fat** –Substantial, generous, lucrative
**Kindling** –Something used to light or ignite
**Replete** –Full
**Bowlines** –Ropes attached to a boat
**Vessel** –A ship or boat
**Chandelier** –An extravagant hanging light fixture
**Chalice** –A large glass used for drinking wine

## LETTER TO LIAM

**Hyperventilating** –Breathing abnormally and at rapid rate
**Chanting** –Repeating rhythmic prayer that is sung by a person or a group of people
**Divine Hymn** –A religious song or poem of God or Gods
**Swoop** –To fly downward quickly

**Tannins** –Plant tissues and substances found in wines
**Sulfur** –A nonmetallic element found in different places in nature. A pale yellow crystalline solid
**Palate** –The roof of the mouth, the part that separates nose and mouth
**Pelting** –Repeatedly hurling something
**Linoleum** –A type of floor covering
**Balthazar** –A large bottle of wine, the big guy
**Krylon** –A brand of spray paint
**Graffiti** –Writings or drawings on wall
**Terrain** –Land or scene
**Lush** –Bright, rich greenery

## I CRIED

**Chords** –A grouping of notes played together
**Agonizing** –Causing great physical or mental pain
**Ghost** –One's own spirit. An apparition
**Snake Charmed** –Charmed by a street performer who makes snakes dance by playing music
**Drawn** –Pulled or dragged

**Atlantis** –A beautiful advanced civilization believed to have sunk into the sea
**Wept** –Cried
**Monsoon** –A very rainy season
**Capsized** –A boat that flips over in water
**Pontoon** –A type of boat
**Imbued** –Drenched
**Exalted** –Praised, worshipped, put on a pedestal
**Indigo** –Dark blue dye
**Somber** –Gloomy
**Koi Fish** –A bright orange fish of the carp family, bred in Japan
**Boisterously** –Noisy
**Dew** –Tiny drops of water
**Rambunctious** –Uncontrollable
**Typhoon** –A tropical storm
**Aquamarine** –A precious stone that is light bluish-green
**Wailed** –Cried loudly
**Poseidon** –The God of the Sea
**Gargantuan** –Enormous
**Third Eye** –Inner eye, spiritual eye, You
**Irises** –The colored part of one's eyes
**Subsided** –Calmed, relented, eased up

## TRAFFIC LIGHTS

**Quasar** –A massive celestial object that emits large amounts of energy such as a star
**Orbit** –The curved path of a celestial body such as star, planet and moon
**Cosmic** –Of or relating to the universe
**Havoc** –Destruction

## LIGHT

**Eon** –Long period of time
**Progeny** –Offspring
**Incandescent** –Glowing white with heat
**Aura** –The soul
**Chimerical** –Imaginary
**Prism** –Object that disperses light
**Zenith** –Point of the heavens directly over a person's head
**Phoenix** –Mythological bird that rose from its own ashes
**Encrusted** –Encased, outwardly covered
**Aesthetic** –Sensitive to beauty, philosophy of beauty
**Affluent** –Abundant, prosperous
**Reverie** –Lost in thought; dream
**Enamored** –In love

**Kiss** –When lips come together to separate bodies and merge the souls
**Shards** –Slivers of something broken into fine pieces
**Omni** –All
**Photosynthesis** –Process used by plants to convert sunlight into usable energy
**Catharsis** –Purging of emotions through expression
**Oolong** –A brown or black Asian tea
**Inundated** –Flooded
**Ambience** –Pervading atmosphere; mood
**Chrysalis** –Cocoon; metaphoric phase such as between caterpillar and butterfly

## FOREVER WAITING

**Illusive** –Deceptive
**Tethered** –Tied down as with a rope or chain
**Sundial** –An old clock used for telling the time of day by a marker that casts a shadow
**DeLorean** –The car used as a time machine in the movie *Back to the Future* starring Michael J. Fox
**North Star** –The brightest star in the sky, also known as Polaris

**Pegasus** –A mythological winged horse. A constellation
**Primordial** –From the beginning of time
**Choir** –A group of singers
**NASA** –National Aeronautics and Space Administration
**Papyrus Scrolls** –Ancient Egyptian material used as paper, rope and other materials
**Carcass** –A dead animal body
**Wading** –Walking through water

NEW WINE

**Goose Ridge** –An area located in Eastern Washington's wine country
**Plodding** –Stomping, trampling
**Gleaning** –Taking, drawing, extracting
**Painstakingly** –Carefully, diligently
**Granite** –A hard granular surface
**Utterly** –Completely
**Rapt** –Fascinated
**Wine Skin** –An old wine container made from animal skin

ODE TO GRAPE

**Bulbous** –Fat and bulging
**Galaxy** –A system of billions of stars
**Plump** –Chubby, fat, ample

**Pinot Noir** –A variety of grape, a black grape
**Adore** –To love and respect something deeply
**Gorgeous** –Beautiful
**Drooping** –Hanging downward
**Tulips** –Spring flowers
**Pinot Gris** –A variety of grape, a green grape
**Kismet** –Fate, destiny
**Serendipity** –Coincidences of a beneficial nature
**Migrant Workers** –Workers that move due to seasonal work
**Pesos** –The currency of Mexico and other Latin American Countries
**Cleavage** –The hollow space between a woman's breasts
**Scarlet** –A bright red color; immoral
**Goddess** –A female deity
**Marauding** –Looting
**Merlot** –A grape variety, a black wine grape
**Lingerie** –A woman's undergarment
**Climax** –An intense excitement; orgasm
**Patter** –A continuous, light tapping sound.
**Crimson** –A deep red color
**Succubus** –A female demon
**Jezebel** –An immoral woman
**Hobos** –Homeless people

**Delicate** –Intricate, fragile
**Mother Teresa** –Roman Catholic nun, known for her work with the poor
**Mary Magdalene** –A follower of Jesus Christ; prostitute in the Holy Bible
**Noble** –Righteous, virtuous, good
**Serum** –A clear portion of any liquid that has been separated from its other solid elements
**Sauvignon** –A grape variety, a green grape
**Mystic** –A spiritual or religious person, paranormal, metaphysical
**Summoned** –Sent for
**Meek** –Tame, submissive, obedient
**Placid** –Calm, serene, composed
**Sacred** –Holy, blessed
**Hallowed** –Holy, blessed, revered
**Withering** –Becoming dried and shriveled
**Asunder** –Divided into small parts and pieces

## BEYOND THE CRUSH

**Scantily-clad** –Insufficient clothing
**Petit** –Small. A grape variety
**Plains** –Prairies, country sides
**Sleazy** –Immoral
**Riesling** –White wine
**Kama** –The God of Love

**Scarlet** –Bright red color, immoral woman
**Starlet** –A young actress striving to become a star
**Wallow** –To roll about, indulge in something
**Thralls** –Being in someone's power or having power over someone
**Alsace** –A region in NE France
**Pistil** –The female organs of a flower
**En Fuego** –Hot, fire
**Tango** –A Southern American ballroom dance
**Sangria** –A Spanish red wine
**Decant** –To pour wine into another container to allow oxygen to open up the wine so that flavors and aromas escape
**Kerosene** –Fuel, a characteristic often detected in Rieslings
**Canteen** –A small water bottle
**Maverick** –An independent thinker
**Noble Rot** –A deliberate process in grape production that enhances certain characteristics in wine
**Constance** –A place in Germany
**Spasm** –An involuntary muscle convulsion
**Double entendre** –A word or phrase that has double meanings
**Mantra** –A phrase or word repeated over and over in prayer or meditation.

**Frank Sinatra** –Singer and Actor
**Brut** –A Dry Champagne
**Tussling** –Struggling or scuffling

MOONSHINE

**Surveillance** –Close observation, security watch
**Corona** –A visible gaseous ring around the Sun or Moon
**Splayed** -Spread out
**Nab** -To steal

SHE'S FLY

**Raphael Santi** –A great Italian painter from the Renaissance era
**Michelangelo** –A great Italian painter from the renaissance era
**Unison** –In harmony
**Pollinating** –Fertilizing a flower
**Transparent** –See-through
**Watts** –Units of power
**Levitating** –Floating in mid-air
**Gallops** –Sprints in a trotting motion
**Crept** –Advanced to a point slowly
**Sever** –To cut off
**Unfurl** –To spread one's wings

## WORKIN' MY WAY UP

**Stilettos** –High heels
**Harem** –Women's quarters, a place for concubines to work
**Harlots** –Immoral women, prostitutes
**Smother** –To suffocate
**Fondue** –A dish where bite-sized foods are dipped into a sauce
**Sedate** –To calm or dull
**Kama Sutra** –Art of love and sexual techniques
**Studious** –Spending a lot of time studying
**Prude** –A person who is extremely shy when it comes to the subject of sex
**Prudence** –Caution, care about ones plans for the future
**Mosh Pit** –A style of dance found in front stage at rock concerts
**Sake Bomb** –Sake is a Japanese Rice wine, Sake Bomb is a drink served at some bars and night clubs
**Mirage** –Optical illusion
**Inny** –A belly button that sticks out rather than in
**Shawshank** –Referencing the hit movie *The Shawshank Redemption*
**Warden** –The head supervisor of a prison
**Extorting** –Obtaining something by force or threat usually money

**Che** –A revolutionary, Guerilla leader
**Ghetto Blaster** –A large stereo that was often the main source of entertainment in some urban neighborhoods in the 1970s and 1980s
**Steep** –To soak
**Atomic** –Relating to atoms or the atom bomb

## FORTUNE

**Deserted** –To be stranded
**Vow** –To promise
**Honor** –Respect
**Sustenance** –Nourishment
**Grand** –Magnificent
**Grandeur** –Magnificence
**Indigence** –Poverty
**Firearms** –Guns, weapons
**Ornament** –Trinket, doodad
**Solar plexus** –The nerves meeting between the stomach and heart; one's guts

## ANOTHER GIGANTIC DREAM

**Recurring** –Happening over and over again.
**Colossal** –Gigantic, very large
**Cypress** –An evergreen tree
**Pygmy** –Very short people of an African tribe

## THE ICARUS ODE

**Icarus** –Mythological character. Had wings made from wax and feathers. He was warned by his father not to fly to close to the sun or his wings would melt off.
**Grizzly** –A large bear
**Defy** –Refuse to obey
**Crane** –Stretch out one's own neck
**Idling** –Inactive, on standby
**Chakra** –A center on the body with spiritual power
**Nike Swoosh** –The branding of Nike
**Aviator Cap** –A pilot's hat
**Manifest** –To show or reveal something
**Chemtrails** –The long smoke trails that jets leave behind in the sky
**Dissipate** –Evaporate
**Borne** –Carried or transported by something
**Khalil Gibran** –Poet, writer and artist
**Messiah** –A savior
**Pulley** –A wheel-type mechanism
**Piston** –A valve of an engine
**Tarp** –A sheet or cover
**Sheer** –Pure
**Will** –Determination, mind power
**Pulsing** –Heartbeat

**Propellers** –Spinning blades of a helicopter or jet engine

Please share this book.

# Thank You!

## BOOK JORDAN CHANEY

Jordan Chaney
is available for booking.

Workshops, Speaking Engagements,
Performances and Poetry Readings.

## CONTACT:

jordanchaneypoet@gmail.com

**www.BillowingWords.com**

Facebook.com/JordanChaney

## WANT MORE?

www.youtube.com/
TheJordanChaneyShow